AF207176

IMAGES
of America

MONTEZUMA CASTLE NATIONAL MONUMENT

This sign, which once informed visitors that they were one mile from the monument, was posted along the access road to Montezuma Castle in 1950. (Courtesy National Park Service.)

ON THE COVER: This 1924 photograph shows the four ladders used to climb up to Montezuma Castle. This was the only way visitors could gain access. (Courtesy National Park Service.)

IMAGES
of America

MONTEZUMA CASTLE NATIONAL MONUMENT

Rod Timanus

ARCADIA
PUBLISHING

Copyright © 2014 by Rod Timanus
ISBN 978-1-4671-3187-2

Published by Arcadia Publishing
Charleston, South Carolina

Printed in the United States of America

Library of Congress Control Number: 2013955107

For all general information, please contact Arcadia Publishing:
Telephone 843-853-2070
Fax 843-853-0044
E-mail sales@arcadiapublishing.com
For customer service and orders:
Toll-Free 1-888-313-2665

Visit us on the Internet at www.arcadiapublishing.com

*To those who built it, to those who struggled to preserve
it, and to those who maintain it today.*

CONTENTS

ACKNOWLEDGMENTS

First and foremost, I must thank Alyssa Jones, acquisitions editor at Arcadia Publishing, for bringing this fascinating subject to me. I must admit that I probably would not have delved as deeply into this aspect of history otherwise, and that would have been my loss. Along my research path, I met many people who deserve recognition for their aid and interest in my project. The staff at the Sharlot Hall Museum archives in Prescott, Arizona, was extremely kind and courteous during my visit there. Park guide Krystina Mucha ushered me through the Tuzigoot National Monument archives with grace and good humor, and Matt Guebard, park archeologist for both Tuzigoot and Montezuma Castle, fielded my many e-mailed questions and accepted my amateur observations warmly and professionally. His observations on the artwork I created for this book were invaluable in assuring the accuracy of my work. A special thanks must be extended to Josh Protas, author of the informative book *A Past Preserved in Stone: A History of Montezuma Castle National Monument*. After I tracked him down in Washington, DC, where he now works, he offered his expertise and advice over the phone and via e-mails. Lastly, to the friends, acquaintances, and colleagues who invariably greeted me these past many months with "How's the book coming along?" I can now gratefully reply, "It's done and thank you all!"

INTRODUCTION

There were people living in the place now known as Arizona 12,000 years ago. Called Clovis today, these people left behind scant evidence of their passing, other than stone arrowheads and spearheads. The people who came after are known as the Ancient Ones. They hunted the mountains and deserts, fished the rivers and streams, dug irrigation canals and planted crops to sustain themselves, and built homes and communities. Then, they mysteriously vanished. Their haunting imprint upon the land—crumbling stone ruins, traces of hand-dug canals, and empty cliff dwellings—stands in silent testimony to their passing. They are known today as the Cochise, the Anasazi, the Hohokam, and the Sinagua. The inheritors of their legacy live today in Arizona as the Pima, the Papago (Tohono O'odham), the Navajo, the Yavapai, and the Apache.

The Sinagua people left behind a singular structure, and this part of their legacy has captured the imaginations of countless people who have looked upon it over the years. The cliff dwelling those ancient people built, overlooking the Verde Valley, is the most complete example of their handiwork in Arizona. Other large Sinagua structures remain throughout the area, but they are only shadowy ruins of what they once were.

The story of Montezuma Castle National Monument has been over 900 years in the making. It begins with an ancient unsolved mystery, chronicles dedicated individual efforts to preserve and protect the site, and continues with modern-day triumphs of careful management aimed at achieving that goal. This story spans centuries, cultures, and attitudes. It is at once a tale of the past and of the future, and of the tangible connection between the two that binds us together as the human species.

The story begins . . .

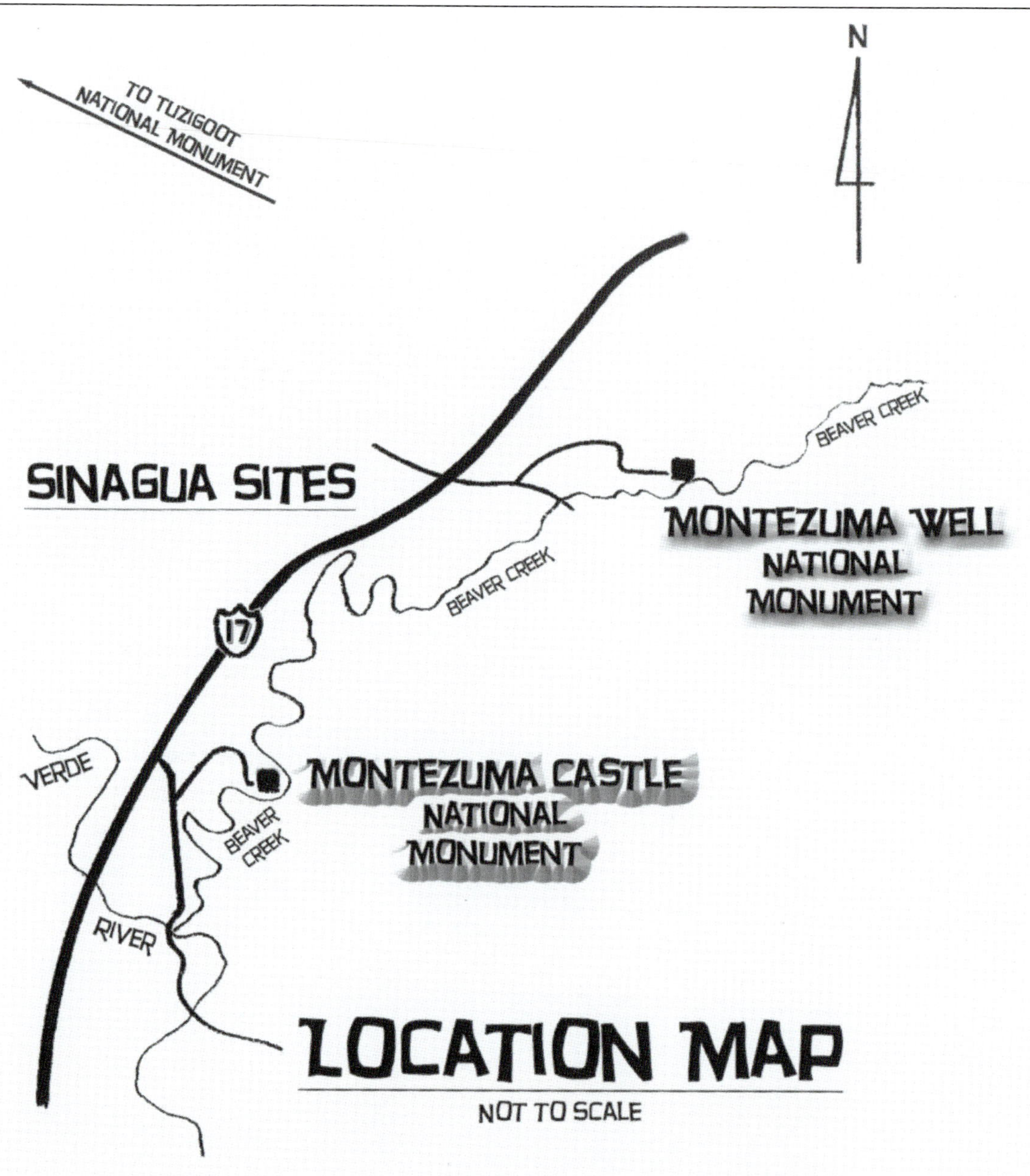

This map shows the Montezuma Castle site in relation to the Montezuma Well site. The Castle is located in Camp Verde, exit 289 off I-17, and the Well is near the town of Rimrock, exit 293. The two sites are 11 miles apart. (Author.)

One

THE SINAGUA

The Hopi call them Hisat'sinom, which means "People of Long Ago" or "Mystery People." Modern researchers, historians, and archeologists refer to them as the Sinagua, a Spanish name for the northern San Francisco Peaks area in which a portion of the group lived, Sierra de Sin Agua, or "Mountains without water." In the 1930s, the name Sinagua was applied to them as a people and continues to this day, even though the region they lived in was far from arid. What they called themselves will never be known.

What is known about them comes from the evidence they left behind. The Sinagua culture flourished from the 7th to the 14th centuries A.D. in large areas of present-day Arizona. They were divided into two distinct territorial groups. The Northern Sinagua inhabited the San Francisco Peaks area near and east of modern-day Flagstaff. The Southern Sinagua occupied the Verde Valley region to the south, near the current towns of Camp Verde, Cottonwood, and Sedona.

In the Verde Valley, the Sinagua were successful farmers who dug an intricate series of irrigation ditches, an art they borrowed from their Hohokam neighbors to the south, to nourish their crops. They cultivated fields of corn, squash, beans, and cotton to sustain them. As with native peoples everywhere, they also used local plants for food, medicines, dyes, and apparel. Sporadic hunting provided the meat of rabbits, deer, and duck to supplement their diet.

The Sinagua were proficient builders, too, using construction techniques influenced by the Anasazi people to the north. Utilizing native wood and stone, they created community dwellings that could house 100 or more people at a time, as well as individual family homes. The ancient remains of their building activities stand today as a testament to their tenacity and to their construction methods. Most notably, the structures at Walnut Canyon, Tuzigoot, and Montezuma Castle bear witness to the ingenuity of a people in harmony with their environment.

The men who helped create those monumental structures stood a mere five feet, four inches tall on average and were of a thin yet muscular build. The women were barely five feet in height but were as hardy as the men. Males wore a simple loincloth of woven cotton, and females dressed in plain shifts of the same material, worn off one shoulder, in the cooler months and a plain string-type skirt fashioned from cotton or yucca fibers in hotter weather. Both wore sandals fashioned of twisted yucca leaves. Their daily routines, when not erecting stone structures in which to live and store food, included such activities as planting and tending crops, hunting small game, grinding and cooking corn and other foodstuffs, weaving cotton fabrics, flaking small stone arrowheads and spearheads, modeling and firing plain, unadorned clay pottery, and teaching the children those essential survival skills.

Evidence suggests that they were a spiritual people, but they did not overly decorate their homes with pictographs, painted images, or petroglyphs (images carved into stone). Near present-day Sedona, however, over 1,000 petroglyphs were found in one place, indicating that the site held a special, even religious, significance for the Sinagua. Their homes were considered just shelter. They even buried their dead in the floors of their dwellings without much of a ceremony other than facing the head of the stretched-out deceased in a certain direction and placing a few important items with it. Residents of upper chambers buried their dead as close as possible to the home in solid ground.

Over the centuries, as the Sinagua region grew and prospered, so too did their interaction with surrounding groups. Their home territory became part of a vast intertribal trade network. Shells from the Pacific coast came into their possession, as did brightly colored parrots from as far away as northern Mexico. Sinagua weavings and pottery went out to other regions in return. They domesticated dogs and turkeys, tilled the soil, traded for goods from far-flung locales, and lived in peace with their neighbors. For 300 years, they maintained their way of life in and around the lush Verde Valley.

Then, around 1400 A.D., the Sinagua simply began to pack up and leave it all behind, never to return. They departed not in a flood but a slow seepage that gradually emptied their territory. Theories abound today as to the cause for their departure, but none precisely fits the historical record. No scholar has yet produced a satisfactory reason to explain why nearly 5,000 people, the estimated population at the time the exodus began, would abandon everything they had known for centuries and go somewhere else over 50 years before Columbus landed in the New World. But go they did.

The "Mystery People" have lived up to their Hopi name. They may have vanished from history, but they left clues of their existence for future generations to ponder, interpret, misinterpret, reinterpret, and simply marvel at.

This drawing depicts a Sinagua farmer with a digging stick commonly used to gouge out furrows to plant seeds. He wears a cotton loincloth and yucca sandals. (Author.)

A Sinagua woman is depicted grinding corn in a *metate*, or grinding bowl. The ground corn will be placed in the clay pottery jug at her side for storage and later use. She wears a one-piece woven cotton shift commonly donned in cold weather. (Author.)

Shown here are the remains of a Sinagua irrigation ditch, photographed in 1962. Over the centuries, as water rich in limestone deposits flowed through the ditch, the mineral clung to the sides and bottom, creating a hard, concrete-like coating. (Courtesy National Park Service.)

A clay pot (left) and a metate (right) were uncovered and photographed in place at the Montezuma Castle National Monument Castle A site during a 1934 excavation. (Courtesy National Park Service.)

A reconstructed clay pot is
exhibited at the Tuzigoot National
Monument museum. Note the
similarity to the pot in the 1934
excavation photograph on the
previous page. In both cases,
the neck is slightly off-center.
Sinagua pottery was plain,
unadorned, and meant only
to be functional. (Author.)

A metate and a grinding stone
are shown here on display at
Montezuma Castle National
Monument. (Courtesy
Barbara Prichard.)

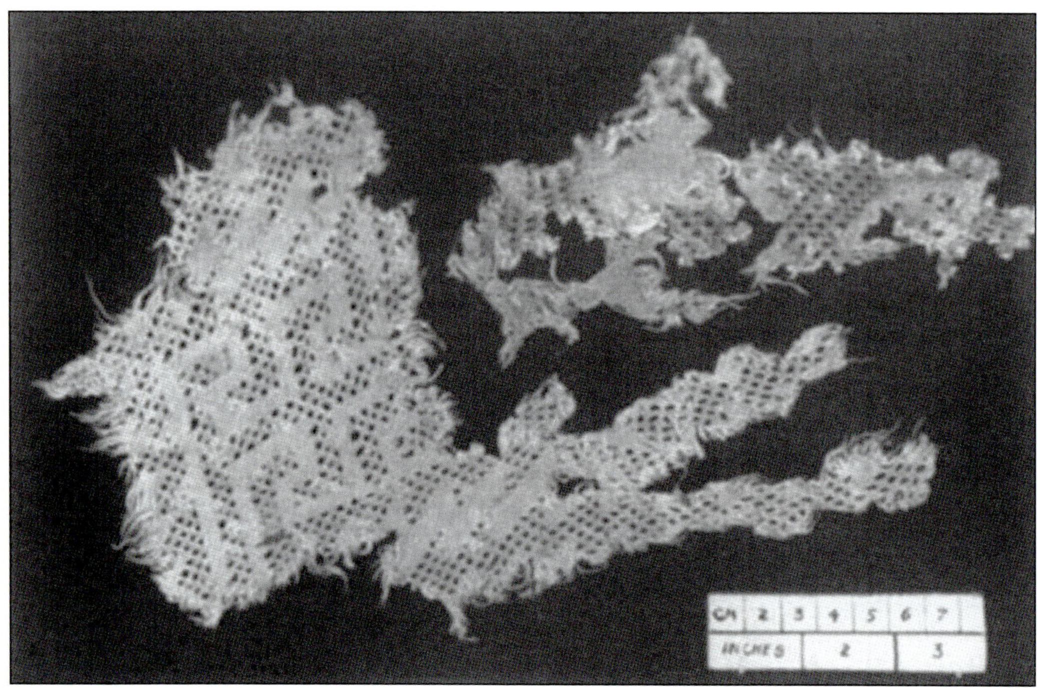

This is an example of Sinagua corded cotton fabric weaving. (Courtesy National Park Service.)

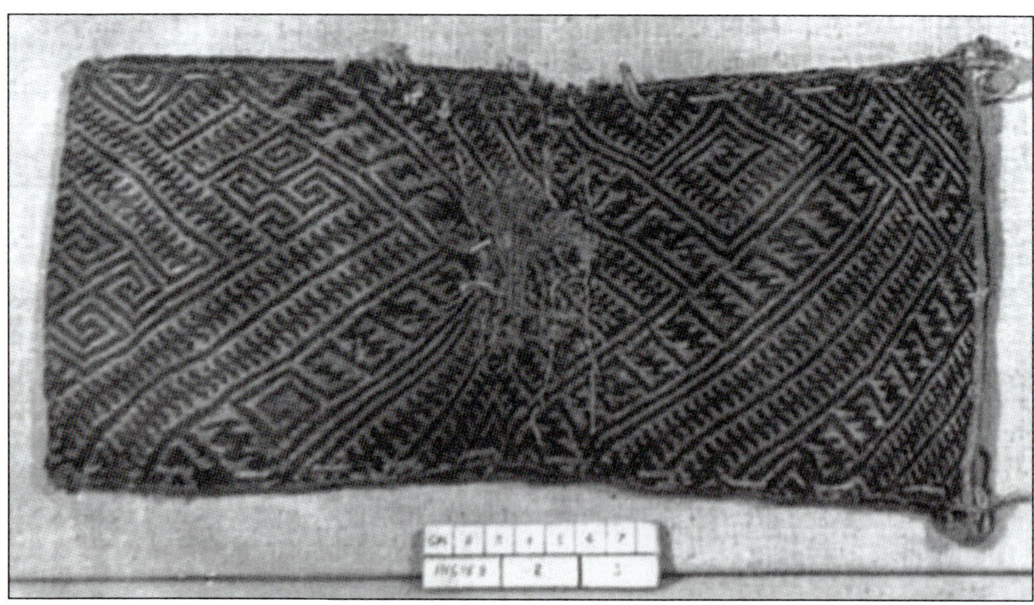

This woven cotton bag with decorative weaving may have been meant to be used in trade. The Sinaguas' territory was situated on a major trade route, and they traded goods with groups as far away as the Pacific coast and present-day northern Mexico. (Courtesy National Park Service.)

Yucca-leaf sandals were worn by both Sinagua men and women. The women also used the leaves of the yucca plant to create skirts for wear in the summer. (Courtesy National Park Service.)

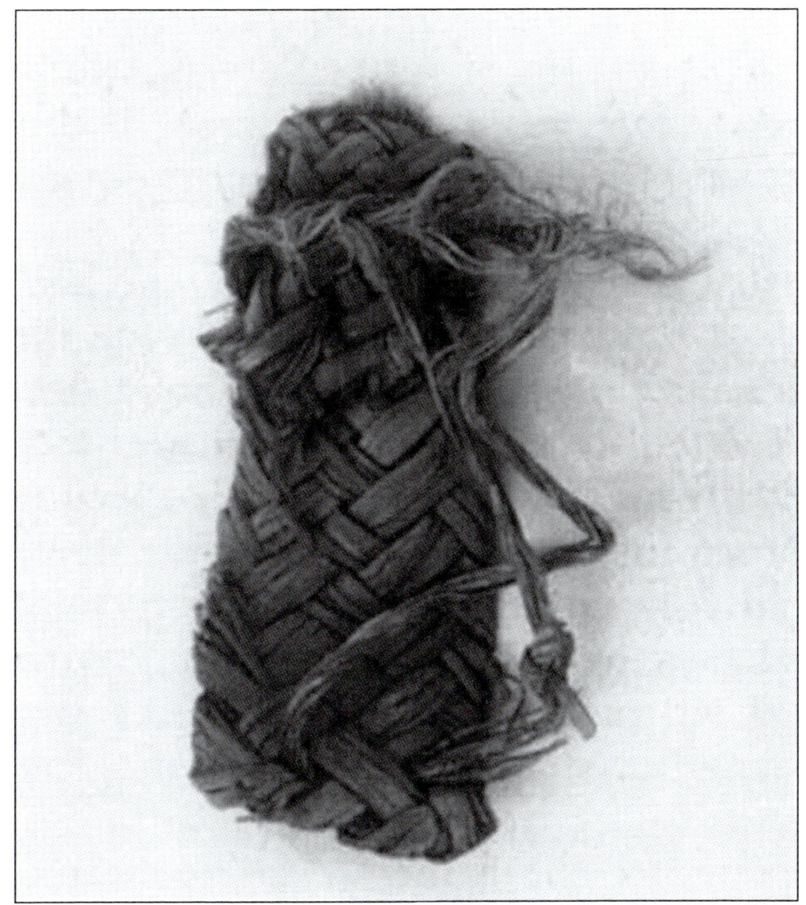

These are Sinagua artifacts unearthed at Montezuma Castle National Monument. They include a piece of gourd with its curved handle, a small squash, raw cotton bolls, a spindle, and corn kernels. (Courtesy National Park Service.)

These stone arrowheads are on display at the Tuzigoot National Monument museum. The Sinagua relied on hunting to supplement their mostly agrarian diet and to provide useful items, like animal bone and sinew, to be fashioned into needles, pins, and rope. (Author.)

Stone axe heads are displayed at the Tuzigoot National Monument museum. (Author.)

This Sinagua couple has set up housekeeping in a walled-in cave. Their "front porch" is the roof of a room constructed below. Their view overlooks the valley and Beaver Creek. (Author.)

In his journal describing his 1583 journey through the Verde Valley, Antonio de Espejo described the ruins his party observed but did not stop to investigate. By that point, the abandoned structure would have begun to show signs of weathering and neglect. (Author.)

Two

MONTEZUMA CASTLE

Sometime around 1100 A.D., Sinagua farmers living at the base of a two-million-year-old limestone cliff in the Verde Valley cast their eyes upward to a large recess about three quarters of the way up a 150-foot escarpment. Soon, they were scrambling up the steep, jagged cliff face carrying hewn Sycamore timbers, baskets of stones, dried reeds, and baskets of mud to begin a monumental structure that would, centuries later, be known as Montezuma Castle. The 20-room, five-story building they created 100 feet above the floodplain of what today is called Beaver Creek would eventually outlast them as a people.

They started small in that cliff alcove; only six rooms were constructed initially. This was probably because there already existed, a short distance to the west, a complex they had built consisting of 45 rooms rising nearly six stories up the cliff face from its base. Construction continued over the years in the lofty location, though, and before long, the original six rooms became the third level of the overall structure as new rooms were added above and below.

Their building technique was simple yet strong and efficient. Stone walls were almost two feet thick at the base and one foot thick at the top, mortared and chinked with mud. Each wall was tapered slightly inward, creating a bowed effect. Tree-trunk roof beams were embedded into the cliff face for strength and extended beyond the wall face. The beams were then covered with interlaced bundles of sticks, small branches, twigs, and reeds laid crosswise. The roof thus formed was then covered with a thick layer of dirt, and sometimes mud, meant to serve as a roof by itself or as the floor of a room above if one were built later. Ceilings were no higher than six feet and doorways no more than five feet in height. Interior doorways between rooms were roughly rectangular, while exterior doorways were shaped like a crude "T" to facilitate ventilation and heat retention.

In 1583, however, a strange new breed of men made their way into the Verde Valley, astride animals never before seen there. The Spaniard Antonio de Espejo led an expedition westward from Santa Fe, New Mexico, on horseback through the Verde Valley. His group rode by the cliff dwelling that had been abandoned over 100 years earlier, but it did not stop to investigate the site. More Spanish expeditions followed, in 1598 and in 1604, but they also ignored the complex and made no note of it in their records.

The Verde Valley was not visited again for 200 years. Then, two American fur-trapping expeditions traversed the valley in 1826 and 1829, seeking beaver pelts to send back East and to Europe to satisfy the market for that fur. Neither expedition left any written records of their travels, so it is impossible to know if the Americans came upon the silent sentinel on the cliff or not. But soon, others would not only discover the site, but would explore it and write about it in detail.

After the Mexican-American War in 1848, which ended with the Treaty of Hildalgo, and the Gadsden Purchase in 1853, the entire area of present-day Arizona came under the control of the United States. American settlers and ranchers streamed in and immediately came into sharp conflict with the native people who lived there. The US Army was soon sent in to protect the settlers and townsmen, building forts and outposts throughout the territory from which to launch campaigns of subjugation against the natives.

During the later years of the 19th century and early years of the 20th century, many individuals and groups worked to protect, preserve, and restore the Montezuma Castle site. When it was designated a National Monument in 1906, six years before Arizona Territory achieved statehood, the federal government assumed those tasks.

Through the 1920s, Frank Pinkley, National Park Service (NPS) custodian of Casa Grande and Tumacacori National Monuments, began to make regular inspection tours of Montezuma Castle as part of his assigned duties. He was appointed to supervise the operations of the Castle in 1921, alongside Martin L. Jackson, who became custodian on a part-time basis. Pinkley and Jackson undertook many major repair and restoration projects as automobile travel brought more visitors to the site. More often than not, the two men performed the work themselves, as no funds were available to hire others. They resurfaced the entire lower section of the Castle, working on ladders precariously balanced on a ledge no wider than three feet while working over their heads. Their aim was always to enhance the experience of visitors touring the complex, although very early on, Pinkley expressed to his superiors his concerns about the continuing damage done to the site by so many people moving through the rooms and the destruction done by vandals when the monument was not open and stood unguarded. Pinkley also petitioned Washington many times to have Jackson named full-time custodian and for permission to have him actually live on the grounds with his family. Finally, the NPS granted permission in 1926, and Martin Jackson built a home at the site that also served as a makeshift museum for many of the artifacts found at the site during the course of his work there. By the end of the decade, the NPS began to authorize several state universities and private organizations to conduct archeological surveys of the Castle and grounds.

The passage of the centuries has done little to lessen the air of mystery and sense of solitude of the place called Montezuma Castle. Its weathered stones have stood in silent witness to the passage of time and have seen changes undreamed of by the people who first laid one stone atop another to build a home for themselves. Even now, when a cooling breeze stirs the leaves in the trees and tall grasses sway like dancers caught up in a slow musical refrain, the voices of those ancient people seem to whisper to the visitor who takes the time to listen, "This was ours, we built it, and now it is yours. Keep it safe. Pass it along to those who will follow you. We are happy you are here."

This is a conjectural drawing of the Montezuma Castle complex. Castle A is on the left, at the base of the cliff. The elevated construction that survives today is on the right. The small cluster of structures at center could have been single dwellings or storage buildings. For nearly 300 years after the completion of the cliff dwelling, the people flourished and prospered in the vicinity. In those years of tranquility, the cliff dwelling became a major landmark in a far-flung trade network that brought useful and exotic items to the inhabitants. Like a beacon to traders from surrounding groups, the structure in the cliff could be seen from many miles away in the Verde Valley. Goods from as far away as the Pacific coast and present-day northern Mexico came into their possession and became part of the lifestyle of the Sinagua. (Author.)

In the *Tenth Annual Report of the US Geographical Survey of the Territories, Embracing Colorado and Parts of Adjacent Territories*, published in 1878, this first known image of Montezuma Castle accompanied an article entitled "Ethnographic Observations by Walter J. Hoffman." (Courtesy Government Printing Office.)

This is a stereogram image card from 1887 showing Montezuma Castle from the east, six years after the famous Gunfight at the OK Corral took place in Tombstone, Arizona. A stereoscope was a hand-held device consisting of two prismatic lenses and a wooden stand to hold the stereo card. When both sides of the card were viewed simultaneously using the stereoscope, the viewer saw a three-dimensional mental image. (Courtesy National Park Service.)

This 1887 image of the cliff dwelling includes Beaver Creek in the foreground, which indicates that the photographer was standing in the water when the photograph was taken. (Courtesy Library of Congress.)

This 1887 photograph encompasses the view of the cliff dwelling. The protective mud coating has long since fallen away from the front facade, where it was not protected from the elements by the cliff overhang above, exposing all the stonework. The inside and outside walls were heavily plastered with the same mud used to hold the stones in place. The dried mud was a natural insulator that kept the structure warmer in the winter and cooler in the summer. Ventilation holes were sometimes punched through a wall, but a larger, window-type opening was extremely rare. (Courtesy Library of Congress.)

For this 1887 photograph, the photographer stood in Beaver Creek. When the water runs low, there are many sandbars and rocky high spots where a tripod can be set up and kept stable and dry. (Courtesy Library of Congress.)

This 1887 photograph, taken from the Castle, shows Beaver Creek running from the right foreground to the center of the image, and the valley beyond. Edward Palmer, the assistant post surgeon at Camp Lincoln in 1865 and 1866, explored the Verde Valley and the cliff site extensively and removed large quantities of artifacts. Although his written notes and descriptions of what he discovered and how he cataloged them survived, his collection of relics disappeared through the neglect and pilferage of someone entrusted with their care. Other visitors soon followed, intending not to explore and document but to plunder and deface the structure. When serious students of history and archeology did visit the site, they found destruction and graffiti left behind by "pot-hunters" and vandals. (Courtesy Library of Congress.)

The Castle is barely distinguishable in this 1888 photograph. It is on the right, in the dark area of the cliff. This photograph was taken from so far away across the valley that Beaver Creek is not visible at all. The photographer appears to have been more concerned with capturing an image of the horse than with the background. (Courtesy Library of Congress.)

This photograph of a horse was taken in 1894. The rider can be seen posing on a ladder just below the Castle on the left. This photograph, and the four that follow, appear to have been taken on the same day. Note the varying degrees of overexposure on the left side of each image. (Courtesy Sharlot Hall Museum.)

This is a view of Montezuma Castle from ground level. Well-intentioned articles written and published in various periodicals by William Manning in 1875, Col. Hiram Hodge in 1877, and William O'Neill in 1887, extolling the wonder and mystery of the ancient cliff dwelling, only seemed initially to attract more uncaring people who were destroying the site a piece at a time. But those same articles also caught the attention of people genuinely concerned with saving and preserving the location. It was during this time that Dr. Edgar A. Mearns, an Army surgeon stationed at Fort Verde from 1884 to 1888, wrote a detailed article about the cliff site. It was published in 1890 in *The Popular Science Monthly*. Mearns used the name "Montezuma's Castle" to describe the structure that was the subject of his extensive investigation. As many had before him, Mearns mistakenly believed that the construction was undertaken by the ancient Aztec people of Mexico. Whatever his reasoning, the name stuck and was used from that time on. (Courtesy National Park Service.)

Fred G. Steenberg is identified in these photographs, taken at the base of the tower in the Castle complex. Steenberg is probably the figure on the ladder in the photograph on page 25, the first in this 1894 sequence. (Both, courtesy National Park Service.)

Shown here is the top-level parapet just beneath the cliff overhang. Steenberg is barely visible at the far end of the parapet wall, just where it gets higher. (Courtesy National Park Service.)

This 1894 photograph documents the efforts to strengthen the upper portion of the tower using boards and cabling to prevent it from collapsing. Note the lintel over a doorway, onto which a ladder leans, on the eastern portion of the complex. (Courtesy National Park Service.)

This 1896 photograph shows that some work has been performed on the eastern doorway since the time of the previous photograph. Layers of stone have been added to return the opening to its original configuration. (Courtesy National Park Service.)

The Arizona Antiquarian Association was formed in 1895 by citizens of the Arizona Territory concerned with the continuing loss of ancient historical sites. From 1897 to 1901, it lobbied territorial legislators to enact laws to protect and preserve those locations, but to no avail. So, in the summer of 1897, using $150 in donated funds, local members of the group undertook repairs and restoration of the Castle on their own. Equipped with 3,000 pounds of materials, including native stones and dirt, iron reinforcing rods, and corrugated sheet metal, they made the perilous climb up to the structure and set to work. This photograph was taken sometime before 1897. (Courtesy National Park Service.)

This pre-1897 photograph shows the boards supporting the top of the tower and a slightly different configuration to the eastern doorway, an indication that stones have either been removed or have fallen away. (Courtesy National Park Service.)

The site is seen here sometime before 1897. Breaks in the walls, some from natural deterioration and others the result of dynamite used by relic hunters, were repaired. Walls in danger of collapse were strengthened and stabilized with supporting rods, and exposed rooms whose roofs had fallen in were covered with metal sheets. Although vandalism and resulting minor repairs at the unprotected site would continue over the next several years, the initial efforts of the Antiquarian Association no doubt saved the structure from total ruin and loss. (Courtesy National Park Service.)

In this photograph, dated 1897, Army officers and their families are on an outing at the Castle. Since nearby Fort Verde was closed in 1891, this group is probably from Fort Whipple in Prescott. (Courtesy Sharlot Hall Museum.)

This illustration appeared in the 1899 book *Montezuma's Castle and Other Weird Tales* by C.B. Cory. The artist fancifully added saguaro cactus at an elevation at which they do not grow in abundance, if at all. (Courtesy Project Gutenberg.)

This photograph of the Castle was taken in 1900, just prior to reconstruction and preservation efforts began in earnest. Visible beside the tower is some sort of dark roofing material, placed atop the long building. (Courtesy National Park Service.)

These two men are standing on the parapet in 1900. The man in the background stands near the spot where Fred G. Steenberg was photographed in 1894. Damage to the room behind the parapet is clearly evident, as is a collapsed portion of the parapet wall in the foreground. (Courtesy National Park Service.)

In the late 1300s, the ground-level complex west of the cliff aerie suffered a catastrophic fire that consumed all the wooden support beams and roofing materials. No longer supported or attached to the cliff face, the entire cluster of structures fell away and crumbled into a massive pile of rubble. Without even bothering to attempt to reconstruct the complex, the people that may have still been there moved away from the area. By 1450, the cliff dwelling was also empty and would never be inhabited again. The site is seen here in 1902. (Courtesy National Park Service.)

This photograph, also taken in 1902 and from the same angle as the previous image, is in sharper focus. It shows the damage to the upper parapet wall, the boards bracing the top of the tower, and the small square opening with a ladder up to it in the eastern portion of the complex (see page 29). (Courtesy National Park Service.)

Another 1902 photograph shows the parapet wall damage filled with stones. Over the years, changes were made to the complex, then undone by other well-intentioned preservationists. Note the hole in the front facade on the left. It started out as two holes, was filled in, then reopened as one large hole. It was eventually reshaped into a single window. (Courtesy National Park Service.)

The repaired upper parapet room is seen here in 1903. The two holes shown in the 1894 and 1900 photographs of the same area have been repaired and turned into small doorways, which probably did not exist originally. (Courtesy National Park Service.)

Theodore Roosevelt (1858–1919) was the 26th president of the United States (1901–1909) when he designated Montezuma Castle a national monument on December 8, 1906, under the Act for the Preservation of American Antiquities, which he had signed into law six months earlier. Montezuma Castle was one of the first sites designated as such in 1906, and it was placed under the joint control of the General Land Office, the Forest Service, and the War Department. (Author.)

This 1906 photograph was taken shortly after Montezuma Castle became a national monument and six years before Arizona became a state. Although 160 acres of land surrounding the site were set aside for federal protection, no funds were allocated to the agencies in charge for maintenance and upkeep. Forest Service ranger Alston D. Morse was assigned to do what he could to ensure the site was accessible and safe for the steadily increasing numbers of visitors, but within the federal administration, the national parks and forests always remained a top priority, and any funds available were channeled there. (Courtesy National Park Service.)

Having just completed climbing the ladders up to the Castle, this 1908 group of tourists pauses to rest and admire the view before exploring the rooms of the complex. (Courtesy Arizona State Library.)

Camping out on the national monument grounds was commonplace in 1909. (Courtesy National Park Service.)

Sharlot Hall (left) and Mrs. L.E. Hewins pose at Montezuma Castle in 1920. Hall (1870–1943) was appointed Arizona territorial historian in 1909, the first woman to hold office in Arizona Territory. She resigned that position in 1912 when Arizona gained statehood. She founded the Prescott Historical Society eight years after this photograph was taken. (Courtesy Arizona State Library.)

Even after the National Park Service Act of 1916 created the National Park Service agency to oversee operations at national parks and monuments exclusively, the parks received the most attention and funding. The monuments were not totally neglected, however, and a major restoration took place at Montezuma Castle in 1917. Alston Morse was hired as a subcontractor for the work, based on his previous experience with the grounds. He undertook the tasks of procuring new ladders for the Castle and making them secure, cleaning graffiti from the interior walls, removing debris, and repairing damage done by looters and souvenir-takers. Montezuma Castle is seen here prior to a major restoration project in 1923. (Courtesy National Park Service.)

This photograph of the tower base was taken in 1923, before restoration began. The worker, posing with his hand on a pre-cut wooden beam, is armed with a pistol in a cross-draw holster. Such a precaution was wise, considering the wilderness area in which the site is located. (Courtesy National Park Service.)

This photograph, taken at the start of the 1923 restoration, shows the scaffolding and braces used to ensure ladder stability while work progresses on the front facade. The wooden boards securing the top of the tower have been replaced with brackets to prevent the tower face from collapsing. (Courtesy National Park Service.)

As the work progressed, ladders and scaffolding were added and removed as needed, depending on what area of the Castle was being worked on. (Courtesy National Park Service.)

As the restoration nears completion, a support beam leans against the cliff face, waiting to be used. A worker at the base of the tower brings another beam up on a pulley. (Courtesy National Park Service.)

All exterior work is completed except for the restoration of the top of the tower and a few cosmetic adjustments. (Courtesy National Park Service.)

This is the only interior photograph taken during the 1923 work. This small doorway was typical of those created by the original builders. Interior restorations and structural bracing were not documented with photographs. (Courtesy National Park Service.)

The top of the tower is seen here, with all support beams removed prior to reconstruction of the floor, roof, and walls. (Courtesy National Park Service.)

In 1924, the restorations were complete except for stuccoing the entire lower facade. The parapet wall has been evened off, the hole in the front has been made into a square window, the small door on the east face has been removed to create a large opening, and the top of the tower has been rebuilt. (Courtesy National Park Service.)

This 1924 photograph shows the placement of the four ladders used to climb up to the Castle. Although the ladders would be replaced with new ones as needed, this was the only way visitors could get in and out of the site. (Courtesy National Park Service.)

These visitors are exploring the site in 1925. The Castle facade, just visible at the top of the photograph, has been completely mudded over, but a portion of the pulley framework used to raise equipment and materials remains in place at the base of the tower. (Courtesy National Park Service.)

This is the cover of the 1928 informational booklet for Montezuma Castle visitors. It was written by Frank Pinkley. Note that the title uses the incorrect possessive "Montezuma's" instead of the correct Montezuma. (Courtesy National Park Service.)

These 1929 photographs show the Castle as it still appears to this day. To date, no suggestion has been put forth of restoring the small doorway on the eastern face, now an enlarged T-shaped opening, to its original configuration. (Both, courtesy National Park Service.)

This is an artist's rendering of what Castle A may have looked like before its destruction. Up to 100 people occupied the site, which predated the cliff construction. Over time, the structures deteriorated under the ravages of weather and a lack of maintenance, and the abandoned cliff dwelling became the home of birds, bats, and all manner of desert creatures. (Author.)

Full-time park custodian Martin L. Jackson is seen exploring a cave in the cliff face above the fallen ruins of Castle A in 1929. Most important to the history of the Castle was Jackson's discovery in 1920 that the massive pile of stone rubble and debris to the west of the Castle location was actually the remains of another large structure. (Courtesy National Park Service.)

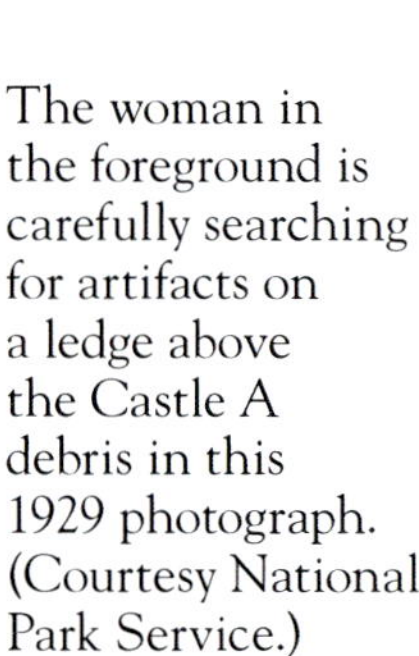

The woman in the foreground is carefully searching for artifacts on a ledge above the Castle A debris in this 1929 photograph. (Courtesy National Park Service.)

This 1933 photograph shows a security device attached to the second ladder up to the Castle. By making sure the ladder cannot be climbed after hours, access to the complex was secured. This also eliminated the necessity of having to remove all the ladders every night. (Courtesy National Park Service.)

In 1933 and 1934, a major excavation project took place at the Castle A site. The removal of rubble and the inspection of the site was performed by workers provided by the Federal Civil Works Administration (CWA), three of whom are shown here. Other CWA projects around the same time included a new parking lot, enlargement of a picnic area, installation of electric wiring and a generator at the custodian residence/museum, and connection of a telephone line. Working with crews from the Federal Public Works Administration, CWA personnel constructed a septic system, a garage for the park vehicle, and a tool shed. (Courtesy National Park Service.)

Shown in the photograph at left are, from right to left, Rooms 2, 3, 4, and 5 after their excavation was completed. The below photograph is an expanded view of the same area. (Both, courtesy National Park Service.)

This photograph was taken at an early stage of the 1933–1934 project. Rubble and debris have been removed from the site. (Courtesy National Park Service.)

The above photograph is a detail of the floor of Room 3, with a storage cave behind it and a work platform just visible above. The slight rise in the foreground is where two infants were found buried under a stone slab. The photograph below shows the same area after excavation, looking east toward the Montezuma Castle location. (Both, courtesy National Park Service.)

Room 3 is described as a burial chamber. Shown here are metates and wooden roof stringers, found when rubble was removed. (Courtesy National Park Service).

After excavation, Room 5 contained metates and a remarkably intact clay pot. (Courtesy National Park Service.)

Room 5 is seen here from a different angle. At right is a circular clay pot firing oven, and on the left are the remains of a wattle (stick and mud) wall. Behind the firing oven is a clay jar called an *olla*. In front of the large pot is a firebox. (Courtesy National Park Service.)

Shown here is the excavation of Room 4. The in-ground firebox in the left foreground was a typical cooking site. The remains of a wooden post are seen behind the firebox. (Courtesy National Park Service.)

Excavation efforts in Room 2 yielded a metate (foreground), a firebox, and remains of a wattle wall. (Courtesy National Park Service.)

A small ledge is seen in an unidentified room, with artifacts in place where they were found. (Courtesy National Park Service.)

The excavation of Room 2 revealed remains of a wattle wall partition base. (Courtesy National Park Service.)

This unidentified room includes remains of walls and a firebox between two post holes. (Both, courtesy National Park Service.)

A worker stands amid Room 4 excavation. Behind him are post holes in the floor. In the foreground is a firebox between two post holes, one with wood protruding. (Courtesy National Park Service.)

Workers reconstructed Room 5 from rubble found at the location. The structure was too unstable to allow public access, and was dismantled shortly after. (Courtesy National Park Service.)

A different view documents the reconstruction work taking place in Room 5. In the left foreground is a remaining pile of stone rubble that has not been removed from the site. (Courtesy National Park Service.)

This is an expanded view of Room 5. The dark area immediately in front of and slightly below the reconstruction are excavated cist graves. A cist grave is a small, flat, stone-lined burial chamber covered with a large, flat stone. (Courtesy National Park Service.)

As pictured here, the 1934 excavations are complete, and the area is cleared of debris. (Courtesy National Park Service.)

In 1935, Dale King created a scale model of Montezuma Castle using clay and plaster. At last report, this model was housed at the Smoki Museum in Prescott, Arizona. (Courtesy National Park Service.)

This 1935 photograph was obviously staged for effect. The ladders have been removed and stacked at the base of the cliff. They are just barely visible above the brush in the foreground and in front of the narrow cave at ground level. (Courtesy Library of Congress.)

This is another 1935 photograph of the Castle. The security device visible on the second ladder, used to prevent unauthorized entry, was still in use. (Courtesy National Park Service.)

In this staged photograph from 1938, the ladders were left in place. It presents a much better representation of what visitors would see. Probably to illustrate the idea of Arizona tourism, the car in the foreground has a California license plate. (Courtesy National Park Service.)

This 1943 photograph shows the makeshift museum and store shortly before its demolition. (Courtesy National Park Service.)

Photographed in 1946, this man has reached the top of the ladder at the base of the tower. He is holding a small child and is climbing one-handed. (Courtesy National Park Service.)

This 1947 group of nine visitors is about to climb up to the Castle with a park guide. By 1940, the National Park Service restricted the number of visitors in a group, out of concern for continuing damage to the site by having too many people in the structure at once. A 25¢ admission fee was also put into effect. Only nine people and one guide were allowed to enter on an hourly schedule. (Courtesy National Park Service.)

The Scott family pauses before their climb to the Castle in 1947. (Courtesy National Park Service.)

This mileage sign to Montezuma Castle was located at the Theodore Roosevelt Dam on the Salt River, northeast of Phoenix. Improvements to local roads and highways brought increases in the number of visitors, slowed only by the outbreak of World War II. After the war, the volume of visitors picked up again dramatically, and the staff found itself hard-pressed to establish programs designed to hold the interest of so many who considered Montezuma Castle an actual destination instead of merely a side trip. This photograph was taken in 1948. (Courtesy National Park Service.)

This is a 1950 sign posted along the access road to Montezuma Castle. The inclusion in 1947 of Montezuma Well, 11 miles distant, into the overall Montezuma Castle complex satisfied historians and archeologists because of its Sinagua connection, but it did little to slow the tide of visitors at the ancient cliff dwelling. To handle the increase in visitors, the monument staff was increased to a supervisor, two park rangers, and a site archeologist. (Courtesy National Park Service.)

In 1951, bowing to the pressure of ongoing damage by tourists and with no other workable option, the National Park Service finally removed the ladders and cut off public access to the Castle in order to save it. From that day to this, only park personnel and qualified professionals are allowed into the interior, for structural inspections and repairs or for scientific study. A large cutaway model of the Castle was installed in a kiosk on the loop trail below the actual complex, allowing visitors to get an idea of how the structure looked on the inside. (Courtesy National Park Service.)

This close-up photograph of the model displays the small Sinagua figures, which were added to the Castle model in 1953 to show the ancient people going about their daily routines within the complex. This photograph was taken in 2013. The model remains unchanged to this day. (Author.)

This 1951 photograph offers a behind-the-scenes look at the only Hollywood Western that featured Montezuma Castle, the Paramount picture *Flaming Feather*. Here, the production team has constructed a set on top of the cliff above the Castle to take advantage of the view. The 1922 Hoot Gibson movie *The Galloping Kid*, from Universal Pictures, featured the Castle in some background shots, but the movie was not filmed on-site. (Courtesy National Park Service.)

This photograph shows the *Flaming Feather* production crew arranging a shot. Cast members and extras are at the base of the cliff and on ladders. The movie starred Sterling Hayden, Barbara Rush, Forrest Tucker, and Victor Jory. Exterior shots were done at the Castle, but interiors were shot on a soundstage using constructed sets, as the real thing was far too small for actors, crew, and equipment to actually work in, on, and around. Other than documentaries, this would be the only feature movie ever shot at the Castle and the only film that used the Castle as part of the storyline. (Courtesy National Park Service.)

Actors and extras wait at the base of the cliff. Production was briefly delayed when local Yavapai extras refused to enter the Castle because of their spiritual beliefs. Navajo extras had to be hired and brought in. (Courtesy National Park Service.)

Action! The US Cavalry charges the Indian fortress while braves fire upon them from above. This fanciful representation of the Castle under attack by the US Cavalry was used on the poster advertising the film when it was released. (Courtesy National Park Service.)

This is the last group of visitors allowed to enter the Castle, in 1951. The ladders were removed that year, and the structure was never again toured by the public. (Courtesy National Park Service.)

The Castle parking lot is seen here in 1956. By this time, the National Park Service developed a master plan for needed improvements to the site and facilities. The most important recommendation in the plan was for a new visitor center, designed to showcase artifacts and information and to handle a larger volume of visitor traffic. (Courtesy National Park Service.)

70

This side elevation plan illustrates the different levels of the structure. It is taken from the 1958 National Park Service book *Montezuma Castle National Monument* by Albert H. Schroeder and Homer F. Hastings. (Courtesy National Park Service.)

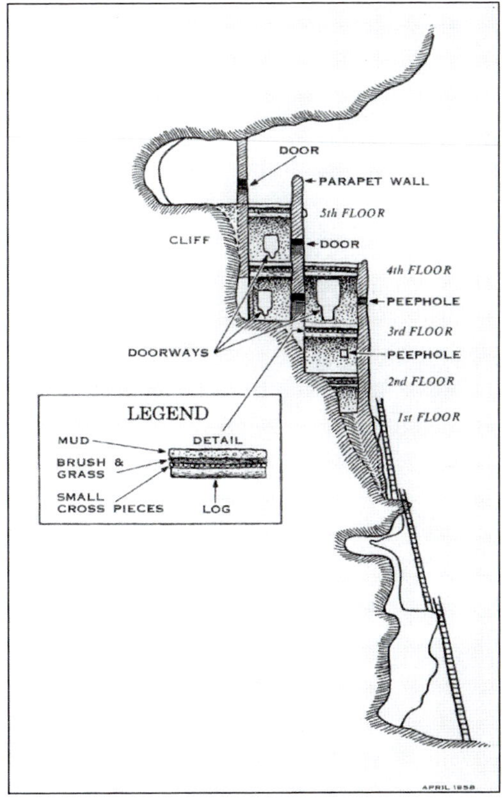

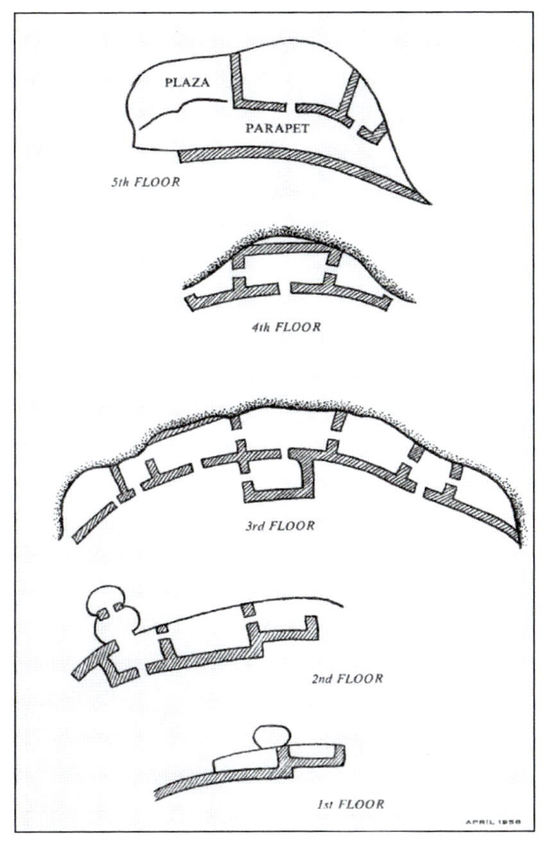

From the same book, these floor plans of each level show the room layouts. (Courtesy National Park Service.)

The model kiosk is shown here in 1959, with the real structure in the background. The benches in the foreground were set up after an informational audio program activated by pushbutton was added to the display. (Courtesy National Park Service.)

In 1960, US senator Barry Goldwater (1909–1998) spoke at the dedication of the new Montezuma Castle National Monument Visitor Center. In 1964, he ran unsuccessfully as the Republican candidate for president. (Courtesy National Park Service.)

The opening ceremony for the 2,500-square-foot visitor center was attended by federal, state, and local dignitaries. Over 2,000 visitors toured the center and monument that day. Included within the new structure were a large lobby, a spacious museum display area, two offices, a gift store, and a utility room. The Montezuma Castle National Monument visitor center is seen here in a recent photograph. (Courtesy Barbara Prichard.)

In 1961, even after Montezuma Castle was closed to the public, visitors could still ascend two flights of stairs to view one of the caves at the Castle A site. The area was accessed by way of an expanded loop trail below the cliff, designed to guide visitors more smoothly beneath the Castle, to the Castle A site, down to the banks of Beaver Creek, and then back to their starting point. (Courtesy National Park Service.)

In 1962, Montezuma Castle National Monument welcomed its one-billionth visitor. In 1966, with the passage of the National Historic Preservation Act, Montezuma Castle was listed in the National Register of Historic Places. (Courtesy National Park Service.)

This 1970 view of the access to the Castle A site shows a portion of a wall built inside the cave (right of center). The public can no longer wander through the site as these visitors are doing. (Courtesy National Park Service.)

A new master operation plan was created for the site in 1975, in keeping with new laws and regulations. However, recommendations for changes contained in it have yet to be implemented to any large degree. Montezuma Castle is seen here in 1975. (Courtesy National Park Service.)

This is a 1983 photograph of Montezuma Castle. (Courtesy Raya Robinson.)

In 1988, a thorough inspection study was conducted within the Castle to check the condition of previous repairs, note any repairs that might be required, and create a comprehensive archeological survey of the site. This 1988 photograph of a hatchway in the ceiling of a Level 1 room was published in the *Archeological Survey and Architectural Study of Montezuma Castle National Monument* by Susan J. Wells and Keith M. Anderson for the Western Archeological and Conservation Center. (Courtesy Digital Archeological Record.)

This is a Level 1 room, showing a cave alcove storage area in the back wall. (Courtesy Digital Archeological Record.)

This is a Level 2 room with structural bracing. (Courtesy Digital Archeological Record.)

This photograph of a Level 2 room
shows a doorway to an adjoining
room and a ladder leading to
the next level. (Courtesy Digital
Archeological Record.)

This view of a Level 3 room shows
how the existing cliff face was
incorporated into the structure
as the back wall. (Courtesy
Digital Archeological Record.)

The Level 3 room above includes a ladder to the next level and a center support beam. At left is a doorway from one Level 3 room to the next. (Both, courtesy Digital Archeological Record.)

The Level 4 catwalk and railings were installed in 1939. As well-intentioned as that installation was, it soon became evident that vibrations transmitted through the walkways anchored to the walls and floors caused more damage to the ancient structure than did regular foot traffic. (Courtesy Digital Archeological Record.)

This photograph of Level 5 shows a small stone bench constructed on the eastern end of the walkway behind the parapet wall. (Courtesy Digital Archeological Record.)

This view of the upper tower "window" includes earlier floor, ceiling, and west wall reconstruction. (Courtesy Digital Archeological Record.)

In this 1990 photograph, the ongoing facade resurfacing by the National Park Service is evident. The upper area, more protected from the elements under the cliff overhang, still has most of its original coating. The lower area, more exposed, has been redone over the years as needed. (Courtesy National Park Service.)

This striking 2004 photograph, showing the view from directly below the Castle, illustrates just how well it has blended in with its surroundings for over 800 years. (Courtesy National Park Service.)

This computer-generated image of Montezuma Castle was created in 2003. It is part of a 20-page entry by a Texas A&M University College of Architecture team in the 2005 Historic American Building Survey of the National Park Service competition. (Courtesy Library of Congress.)

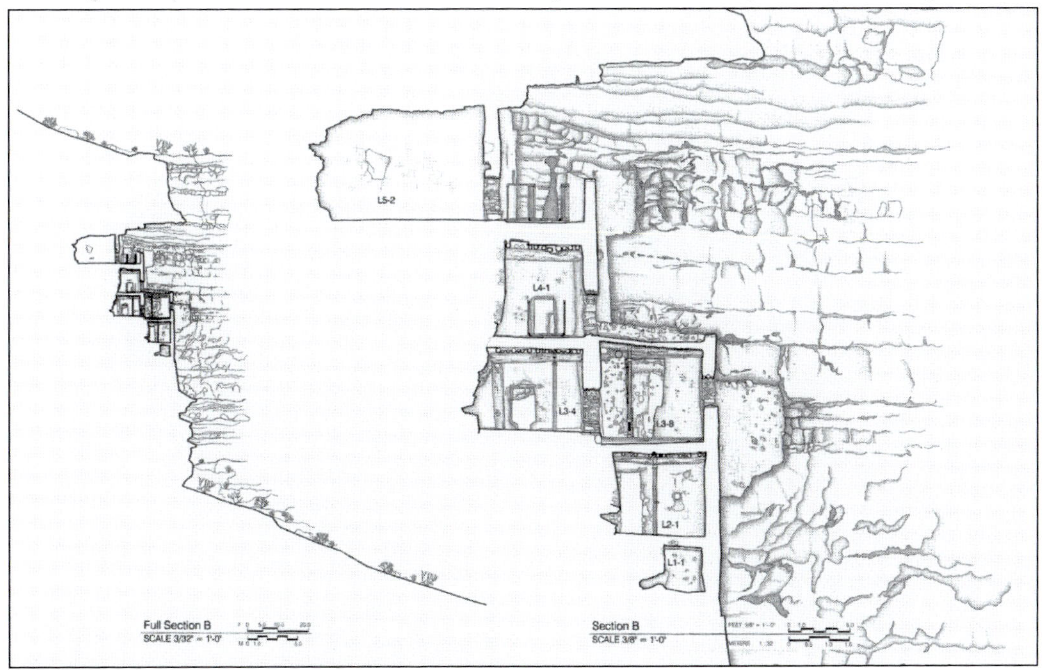

This is a side elevation plan from the same 2005 entry. The Athenaeum of Philadelphia and The American Institute of Architects cosponsored the competition with the National Park Service. The Texas A&M team was awarded second place in the Charles E. Peterson Prize category. (Courtesy Library of Congress.)

In 2006, the Castle reached a series of milestones in its long history. That year marked the 100th anniversary of the passage of the Antiquities Act, the 100th anniversary of Montezuma Castle as a national monument, and the 40th anniversary of the National Historic Preservation Act, which paved the way for the Castle to be listed in the National Register of Historic Places. This photograph was taken in 2006. (Author.)

This 2007 photograph of the tower shows National Park Service facade covering. Behind the tower can be seen the upper portion of the Castle; its original mud covering shows signs of weathering and age. (Courtesy David Rose, www.arizonaruins.com.)

The bottom doorway is the entrance to Level 2, and the doorway at the top leads to the tower Level 3. This 2007 photograph was taken during an annual National Park Service inspection of the Castle. Entry to Level 1 is through the floor of Level 2. (Courtesy National Park Service.)

This photograph, taken from Level 2, looks west toward the site of Castle A, which once stood behind where the trees are now. Perhaps not at all surprising, it appears that the Sinagua women handled a majority of the cliff construction. With the men away every day tending the fields of crops and hunting game, the task of building living quarters would have naturally fallen to the women. It was just one more chore in their daily routines. (Courtesy National Park Service.)

The National Park Service inspection crew is seen entering the Level 2 doorway. (Courtesy National Park Service.)

The area seen in this west-facing photograph is considered Level 3, because it is even with the rebuilt tower room. However, the majority of it is the open roof of Level 2. (Courtesy National Park Service.)

These photographs offer south-facing views of the Verde Valley from an irregular opening in the front wall of Level 2 (right) and from the window created in level 2 during the 1923 restoration project (below). (Both, courtesy National Park Service.)

This photograph looks east from the tower doorway, toward the small doorway that was enlarged in 1923 to allow easier access. It was never restored to its original configuration. (Courtesy National Park Service.)

This is another view of the interior of the same tower doorway, showing the 1923 wall construction that restored and enclosed the upper tower Level 3 room. (Courtesy National Park Service.)

The above photograph, looking south, shows the square opening in the top portion of the tower face. The front wall is original; the side walls and ceiling are reconstructed. The below photograph shows the ceiling construction of sycamore beams and reed thatching, typical of any room in the Castle. (Both, courtesy National Park Service.)

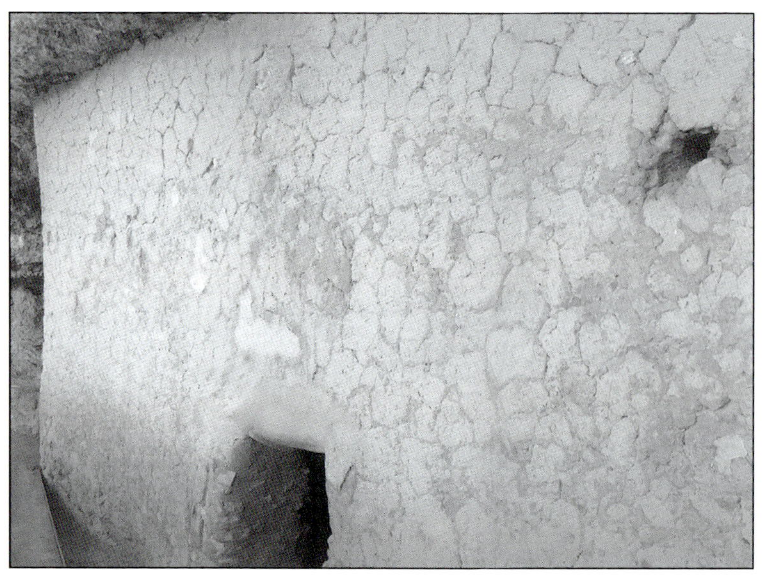

In this Level 4 room is a doorway to the next room. Modern support posts have been installed. Note the names and initials that have been carved into the ceiling beam over the years of public visitation. (Courtesy National Park Service.)

Shown here is the large room behind the parapet on Level 5. (Courtesy National Park Service.)

This photograph was taken inside a
Level 5 room, looking out a side doorway.
Note the smoke-blackened stones,
which remain today from the time the
room was occupied by the Sinagua.
(Courtesy National Park Service.)

This photograph looks down over
the eastern end of the parapet wall
at the eastern portion of the Castle.
(Courtesy National Park Service.)

Taken on Level 5, this photograph looks west toward the site of Castle A. Visible in the foreground, at the bottom right, is a portion of the parapet wall. The roof of Level 2 is seen beyond and below it. (Courtesy National Park Service.)

This view of Level 5 looks west along the parapet wall. The western corner of the Level 5 room is visible, as is the modern catwalk and the top of the access ladder coming up from Level 4. (Courtesy National Park Service.)

This 2013 photograph captures Montezuma Castle from the southeast. Although decidedly nonpolitical in nature and presentation throughout its history, Montezuma Castle has nevertheless been used as a pawn in partisan politics in Washington, DC, in recent times. Federal budget impasses between Democrats and Republicans in 1995–1996 and again in 2013 caused partial government shutdowns that resulted in the closure to the public of the Castle, along with all national parks and monuments around the country, and the furloughing of National Park Service workers. Both impasses were eventually resolved, and the national parks and monuments were reopened. (Courtesy Barbara Prichard.)

Montezuma Castle is seen from the southwest in 2013. (Courtesy Barbara Prichard.)

Here, the 1951 Castle model is superimposed over the actual location. (Courtesy Barbara Prichard and author.)

Three

MONTEZUMA WELL

The geological site today known as Montezuma Well is considerably older than the Montezuma Castle cliff dwelling. In fact, it was several million years in the making. Only the arrival of humans linked the two together.

Over the centuries, bands of Yavapai and Apache, now lords of the Verde Valley, knew of the well and its location, but paid it little heed other than as a landmark to guide their wanderings. Even when the 1583 Spanish expedition of Antonio de Espejo passed through the valley, no mention of the well itself was noted in the record of their trip, other than a brief description of an irrigation ditch and an empty stone building on a hill. From the valley below, the well certainly appears to be just another hill, but imagine their surprise and wonder had they climbed up and beheld what was actually inside. It was not until the Americans arrived in the 1860s that the well was discovered and given any notice.

As conflicts arose between the American settlers and the native people in and around the Verde Valley, raids and retaliation were common among both groups. After one such Apache raid in 1864, King S. Woolsey led a group of settlers in pursuit to exact revenge. As always, the Apache proved an elusive prey, and as the Woolsey expedition was returning empty-handed through the Verde Valley, they came upon the well and explored it. Typical for the time, especially among veterans of the Mexican-American War who had come in contact with Aztec ruins during their conquest of Mexico, any similar-looking ruins in the southwest were assumed to have been created by those ancient people. Woolsey bestowed the name Montezuma Well on the site, and it has since been known by that title.

With the arrival of the US Army to protect the settlers, and the building of forts and outposts in the vicinity, more and more people came to the well for various reasons. In 1866, the same Edward Palmer who had made detailed explorations of Montezuma Castle several miles away explored and wrote about Montezuma Well. By 1870, Wales Arnold, who had a ranch nearby, grazed his livestock around the well, and in 1875, Col. Hiram C. Hodge wrote an article about his exploration of the site. He wrote about finding stone axes and metates in the two cliff houses, of exploring all the rooms in the cave at the well outlet, and of the remains of the great house atop the rim with 20-foot sections of wall still standing. Before long, the well became a popular picnic area for officers and their families from Fort Verde and Fort Whipple, as well as for souvenir- and pot-hunters. The site was soon stripped of all visible artifacts, but it did not suffer the wanton destruction that the Castle did.

By 1883, Sam Shull had obtained squatter rights at the site and claimed the well as part of his property after building a structure and living on the land for a few years. That same year, he traded the property to Abraham Smith for $40 in cash, a pair of chaps, and a horse. Then, two years later, Smith traded his holdings to William B. Back for two horses, bragging that he had doubled his original investment. The Back family retained ownership of the site from 1888 until the mid-20th century.

William Back was an enterprising man. He realized that he had a parcel of land he could farm by utilizing the ancient irrigation ditches the Sinagua had dug. It was also suitable for raising livestock, primarily pigs. In addition, Back knew that he had a genuine tourist attraction with the well site. In 1904, a recommendation was made that the General Land Office purchase Back's property in order to preserve the well site. When contacted in that regard, Back quoted them a price of $2,500 for the 80-acre parcel. The GLO never acted on the deal.

By 1910, Back was giving 50¢ tours of the well, including a rowboat ride on the water with himself at the oars. He was also selling artifacts he had dug up in the ruins and at a nearby burial site from a museum/gift store he had set up in the family home. When William Back died in 1929, his son William Jr. and his wife moved onto the property and continued the tourist operation. He moved the museum into a separate building in 1930. By that time, the Back homestead consisted of the family home and a log smokehouse, along with two caves on the outside of the well that had been cleared and converted into a pigpen and a blacksmith shop. The well itself had benefited greatly by the occupation of the site by the Back family, remaining safe from looters and vandals during that time.

By the late 1930s, the National Park Service was expressing a strong interest in acquiring the Montezuma Well location with an eye toward incorporating it into the Montezuma Castle National Monument as a detached unit. National Park Service inspectors were permitted on the property periodically to assure the government that the site was being safely maintained by the Backs while a sale was worked out. Arizona senator Carl Hayden introduced legislation in the US Congress to authorize the expenditure of $25,000 to purchase the site. Congress approved the price in 1943, but the sum was not paid until 1947 because of the massive national debt incurred during World War II. In 1948, a flurry of activity took place at the well as the National Park Service removed some structures from the property, renovated others, and installed a new water well and pump. Also in 1948, an underwater exploration of the well provided more accurate information about its depth and the configuration of the bottom.

By 1960, two new staff living quarters had been erected at the well, a large shelter was built over the Hohokam pit house, the Swallet Cave ruins were excavated and stabilized, a picnic area was enlarged, and new trailside displays were installed. In 1968, another exploration dive was undertaken at the well, but no report was ever produced. Renovations continued in 1972 with the removal of the 40-year-old museum building erected by William Back Jr., which had become unstable. That year also saw expansion of the parking area and construction of a new ranger contact station at the trailhead of the loop trail. During this period visitation steadily increased, resulting in the necessary changes that were made at the site. There would be no major changes at the well after the replacement of the visitor comfort center in 1981.

In 2006, yet another scientific expedition beneath the waters of the well took place. This exploration, which produced many interesting photographs of the well bottom, was timed to coincide with the 100th anniversary of Montezuma Castle and, by extension, Montezuma Well, as a national monument.

This is an 1887 photograph of Montezuma Well, looking northwest. From two springs on the bottom, water is fed at a rate of over 1,000 gallons a minute, or roughly 1.5 million gallons a day. Had not a fissure 150 feet long through the wall also opened up during the dome collapse that formed the well, allowing 1.8 million gallons a day to flow out, the water would overflow the top. Because the inflow nearly matches the outflow, 13.5 million gallons of water remain inside at all times. (Courtesy Library of Congress.)

This is the Swallet Cave, on the southeast interior wall of the well, just above where the water flows out through the dome wall. Discovered in this complex were nine rooms. In 1895, William Back allowed archeologist Jesse Walter Fewkes to make a detailed study of the well, knowing that any public interest garnered from the report would bring more curiosity seekers. Fewkes was attempting to make a connection between the well and the Hopi people far to the northeast. Even though the Hopi knew of the site and it figured into their mythology, no real connection could be made. This photograph was taken around 1900. (Courtesy National Park Service.)

This 1902 photograph was taken from basically the same angle as the previous photograph. As seen here, debris beyond the small doorway has been removed. A total of seven rooms were excavated inside. (Courtesy National Park Service.)

Shown here in 1907 is the larger of two cliff houses constructed around 1050. They are located near the top of the western wall of the well, overlooking the water. (Courtesy National Park Service.)

This is an expanded view of the cliff dwelling seen on the previous page. Just beyond the right border of this 1909 photograph is another, smaller cliff house built into the same alcove. (Courtesy National Park Service.)

These are the ruins of a large community house structure located on the southeast portion of the dome surrounding the well. It has been estimated that up to 100 people at a time could have occupied this building. This photograph was taken in 1909. (Courtesy National Park Service.)

In this 1915 photograph, William Back, owner of the well and adjoining property, gives visiting tourists a 50¢ tour of the site. The visit included a rowboat ride on the water, with Back at the oars. He sold artifacts he had dug up in the ruins and at a nearby burial site to visitors from a museum/gift store he set up in the family home. (Courtesy Sharlot Hall Museum.)

This 1916 photograph, taken near the well outlet and Swallet Cave, shows William Back conducting a boat tour. At one point, Back stocked the well with fish, but that enterprise failed dismally when the fish suffocated because of the high concentration of carbon dioxide in the water. Visible above the craft are both cliff houses on the western wall. (Courtesy National Park Service.)

This 1947 photograph provides an aerial view of the well. Note the swatch of fertile, treed landscape just outside the site, where the nourishing waters flow out and into the ancient irrigation ditch system and Beaver Creek. (Courtesy National Park Service.)

The cleanup and restoration done by the National Park Service is evident in this 1947 photograph of Swallet Cave. (Courtesy National Park Service.)

In 1948, an underwater exploration of the well was performed. The study provided accurate information about the well's depth and the configuration of its bottom. This diver wears a heavy canvas suit to protect him from the water's cold temperatures. The rope around his waist is secured to the boat he will work from. (Courtesy National Park Service.)

This is a candid photograph of the diver and the boat crew. The machinery in the boat is an air generator, which will pump oxygen through a hose to the diver working below. The depth of the water is 55 feet, and the cliff walls rise another 62 feet from the surface. Because of the temperature of the water entering it, the well never freezes over in the winter. (Courtesy National Park Service.)

Shown here in 1962 is the exterior of the well where the water flows out. From here, the water flows into the series of irrigation ditches the Sinagua dug to divert it to their fields. (Courtesy National Park Service.)

In 1968, another exploration dive was undertaken at the well, but no report was produced. These are the remains of an ancient irrigation ditch in 1962. (Courtesy National Park Service.)

Swallet Cave is seen here during a 1975 inspection tour. Footprints in the dirt are visible near the stones in front of the doorway. (Courtesy National Park Service.)

The large cliff house in the western face of the well is seen here in 1975. Visible at upper center is what appears to be a stabilization wall constructed under a rock outcropping. The wall has clearly done its job for centuries. (Courtesy National Park Service.)

This photograph, taken in 1983 across the well, shows the two cliff houses. At left, visitors can be seen standing atop the rim. (Courtesy Raya Robinson.)

In 2006, divers again probed the waters of Montezuma Well to conduct scientific research. (Courtesy National Park Service.)

A robotic device is pictured near submerged rocks and vegetation debris in 2006. (Courtesy National Park Service.)

The "false bottom" of the well is shown bubbling and roiling in this photograph. A sediment and sand layer ebbs and flows above two large spring openings that pump water into the well on the true bottom. Those openings are between 20 and 30 feet wide. (Courtesy National Park Service.)

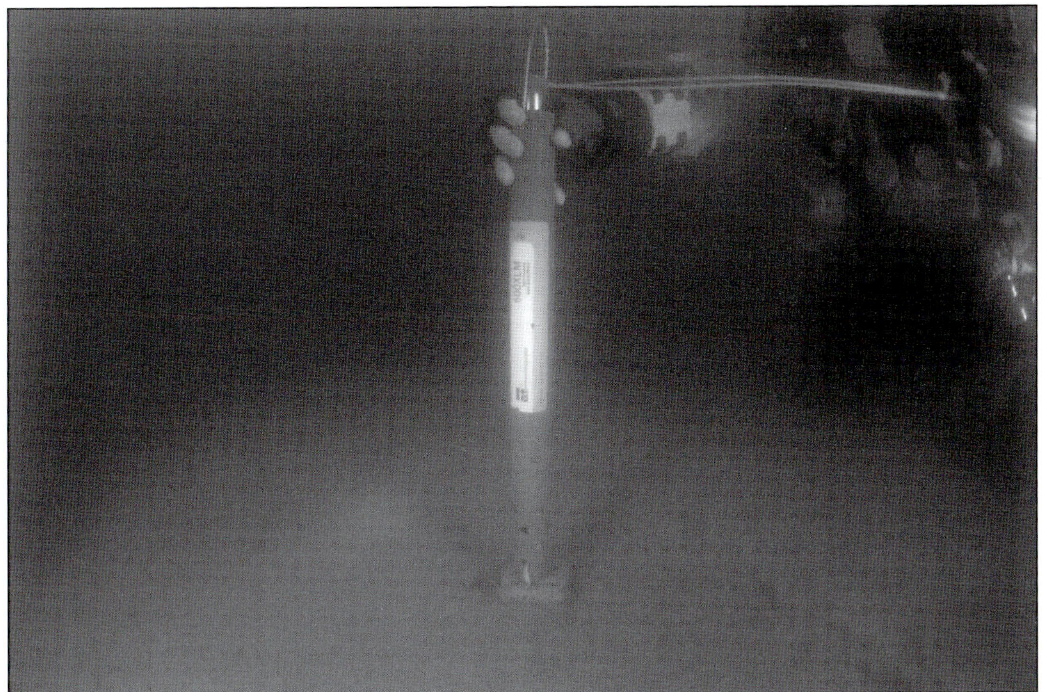

This weighted device is attached to a rope and lowered through the sediment layer until it touches the real bottom, thus producing a measurement of the layer. It is also used to measure the depth of the spring vents that feed the well. (Courtesy National Park Service.)

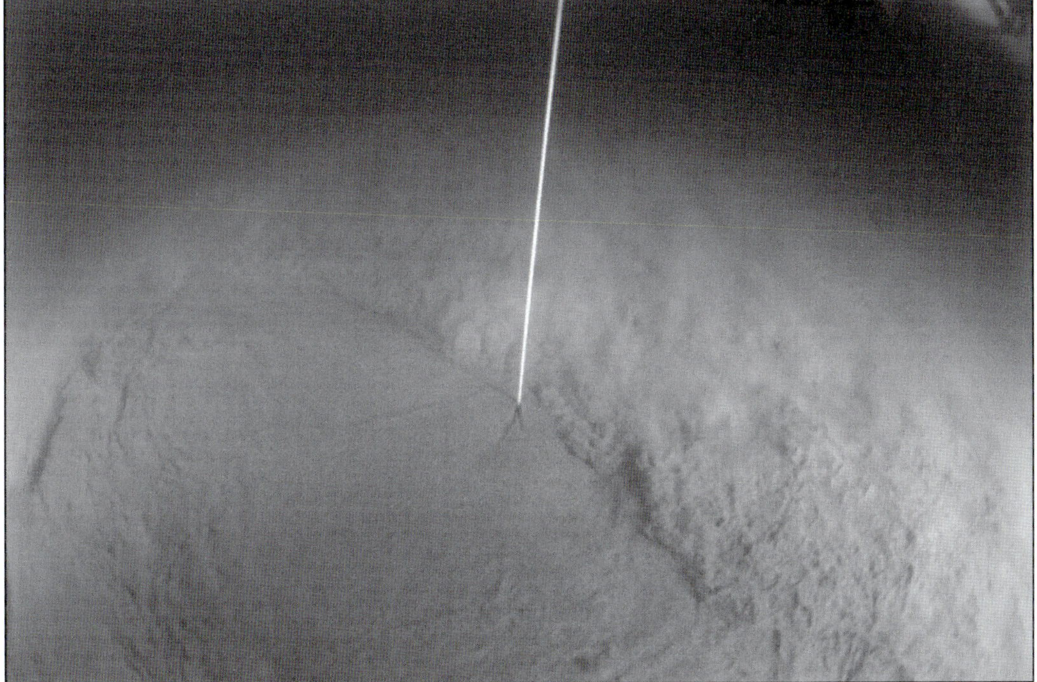

The weight is seen on its way down through the sediment, which enters the well with the water from the springs. (Courtesy National Park Service.)

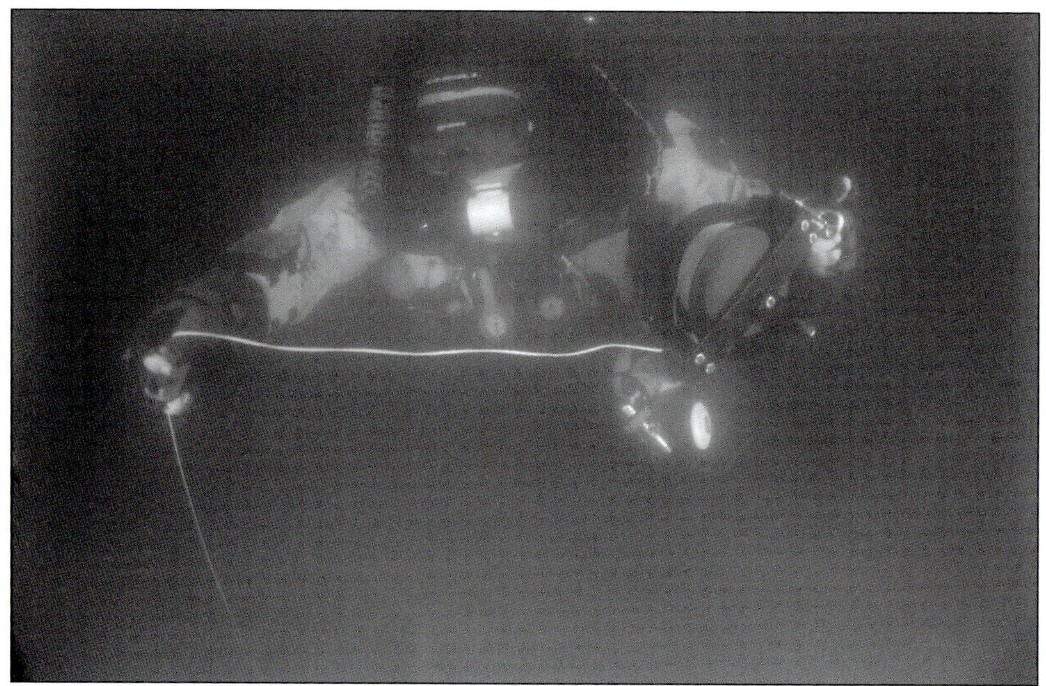

At the other end of the line, the diver plays out the rope until it stops. (Courtesy National Park Service.)

A diver runs his hand through the bottom sediment, which does not cloud up in the water but remains a thick, liquid-like substance. (Courtesy National Park Service.)

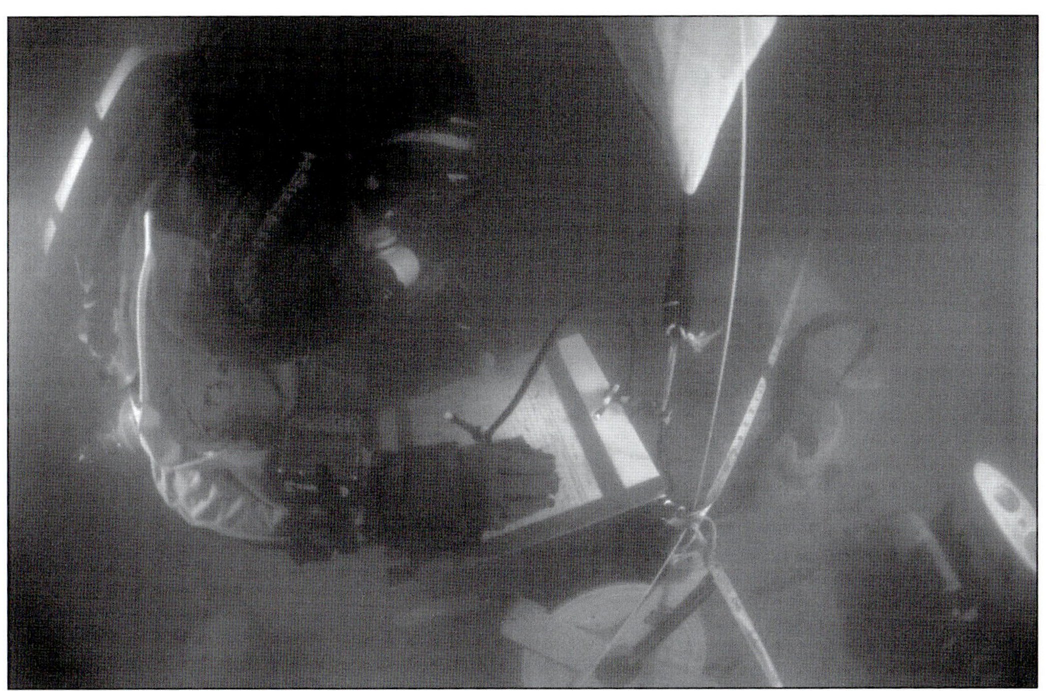

In the above photograph, a diver records information gathered by various scientific instruments brought along by the underwater researchers. Below, he collects rock samples in a plastic container. (Both, courtesy National Park Service.)

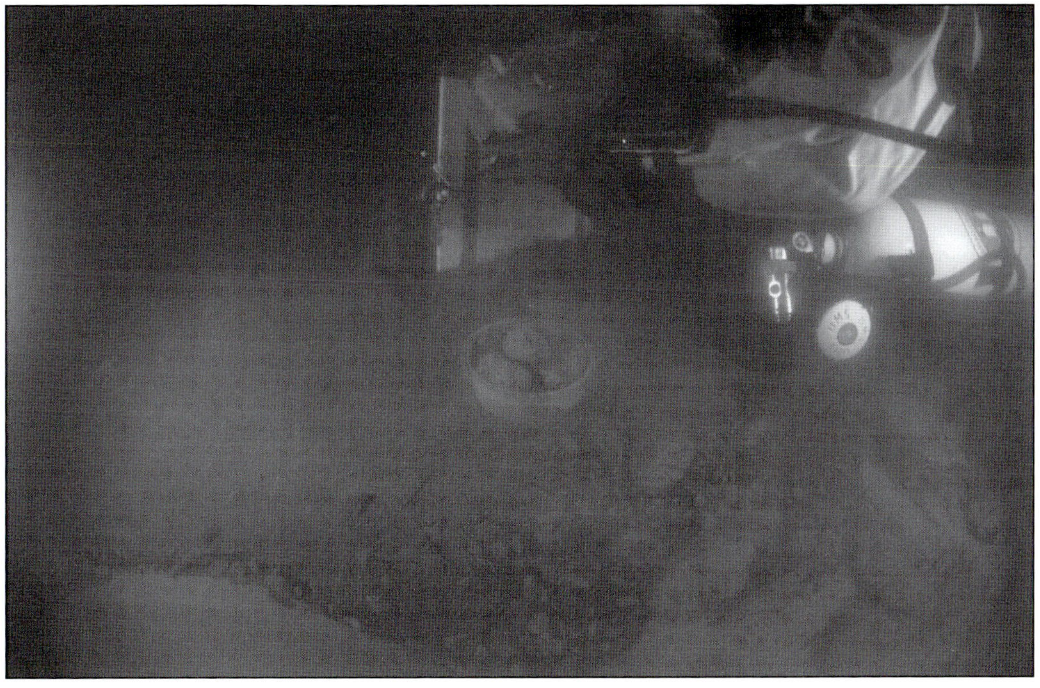

The plastic container is sealed and ready to be taken to the surface. (Courtesy National Park Service.)

A lightweight mesh bag containing collected samples will be attached to a flotation device and brought up from the bottom. (Courtesy National Park Service.)

The diver ensures that his clipboard is firmly attached to a flotation device. Using this method, anything that comes loose on the way up will float to the surface instead of dropping back to the bottom. (Courtesy National Park Service.)

This is an example of the submerged vegetation in the well. (Courtesy National Park Service.)

Construction of a loop trail at the well was completed in 1951, allowing visitors to easily walk up to the rim. From the rim, visitors get not only a panoramic view of the well, but a close-up view of the two cliff houses. In 1952, the trail was extended to the Swallet Cave and the well outlet, accessible by ladder. Stone stairs were installed in 1953, replacing the ladder. This 2013 photograph shows the stone stairs winding down from the rim to the walkway beside the water that leads to Swallet Cave and the outlet where water exits the well. (Courtesy Barbara Prichard.)

In this 2013 photograph of the Swallet Cave entrance, subtle differences can be observed from the 1975 photograph (see page 109). Most notably, the large stone on the ground in front of the entrance has been removed, and other, smaller stones appear in an area that was open. (Courtesy Barbara Prichard.)

Graffiti painted on the wall near the Swallet Cave in 1873 is still visible in this 2013 photograph. It is, in fact, an advertisement for the Rothrock Photography studio in Phoenix. (Courtesy Barbara Prichard.)

Declan Rose reads the informational sign at the well outlet in 2013. From here, the water flows 150 feet through a natural tunnel in the limestone wall to the outside. (Courtesy Barbara Prichard.)

Both of the cliff dwellings at the well are seen here in better detail in 2013. (Author.)

The remains of the community house on the southeast rim of the well are seen here in 2013. (Courtesy Barbara Prichard.)

Shown here is the southeast corner of the community house foundation remains. This building overlooked the northern and eastern Beaver Creek valley below, where the growing fields were located. (Courtesy Barbara Prichard.)

This 2013 photograph of the well was taken looking north across the water from the south rim observation area. The floating objects are turtle traps. A US Geological Survey Southwest Biological Science Center project hopes to capture large numbers of the invasive red-eared slider turtle for relocation, so that the endangered Sonoran mud turtle can be reintroduced at the well. (Courtesy Barbara Prichard.)

This west-facing 2013 photograph shows the cliff dwellings. (Courtesy Barbara Prichard.)

Shown here is the well as it appears today, viewed from the northwest. (Author.)

Ducks swim slowly across the surface of the quiet water of Montezuma Well. Is it any wonder that the Hopi, the Zuni, the Yavapai, and the Western Apache have considered this place sacred for untold centuries? Today, as in centuries past, Montezuma Well stands placid and silent in the Verde Valley landscape, a geologic wonder found nowhere else in the world. Beneath its calm surface, microscopic organisms and tiny invertebrates specially adapted to the acidic environment live out their lives at a frenetic pace that is all but invisible to the casual observer. Montezuma Well is a silent testament to the inexorable power of water and time. It has always been this way, and it will remain so. (Courtesy Barbara Prichard.)

BIBLIOGRAPHY

Blinn, Dean W. *Life Beneath the Water Surface in Montezuma Well, Arizona: A Large Thermally Constant Spring.* Hampstead, MD: Maple Creek Media, 2012.

Lamb, Susan. *Montezuma Castle National Monument.* Oro Valley, AZ: Western National Parks Association, 2003.

Linoff, Lindsay. *The Sinagua People of Montezuma Castle.* Mesa, AZ: Mesa Community College, 1998.

Protas, Josh. *A Past Preserved in Stone: A History of Montezuma Castle National Monument.* Oro Valley, AZ: Western National Parks Association, 2002.

Schroeder, Albert H. and Homer F. Hastings. *Montezuma Castle National Monument.* Washington, DC: National Park Service Historical Handbook Series, No. 27, 1958.

US National Park Service. *Montezuma Castle.* Washington, DC: Department of the Interior, 2010.

Discover Thousands of Local History Books Featuring Millions of Vintage Images

Arcadia Publishing, the leading local history publisher in the United States, is committed to making history accessible and meaningful through publishing books that celebrate and preserve the heritage of America's people and places.

Find more books like this at
www.arcadiapublishing.com

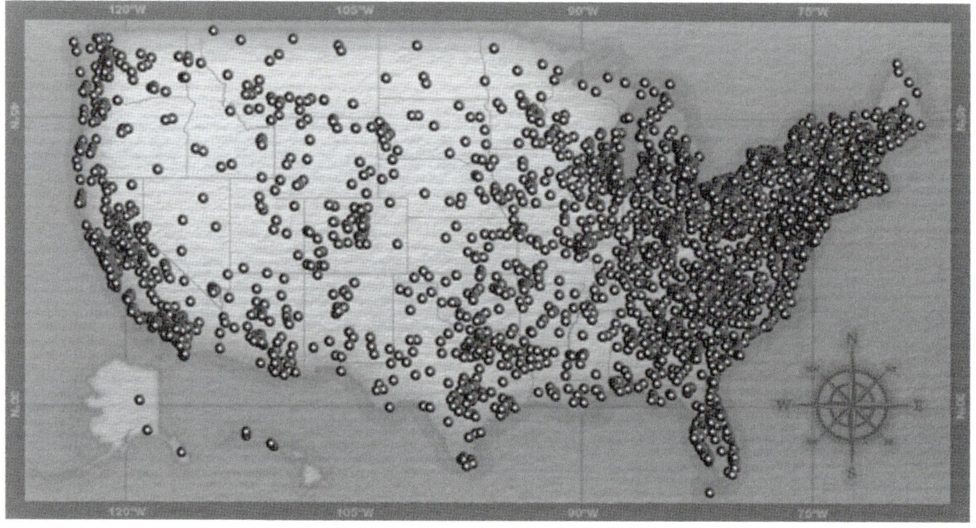

Search for your hometown history, your old stomping grounds, and even your favorite sports team.

Consistent with our mission to preserve history on a local level, this book was printed in South Carolina on American-made paper and manufactured entirely in the United States. Products carrying the accredited Forest Stewardship Council (FSC) label are printed on 100 percent FSC-certified paper.